A recipe for safety

Health and safety in food and drink manufacture

HSE Books

Ingredients

Photograph and drawing acknowledgements:

Allied Bakeries
Panacea Gold Ltd
Dairycrest Ltd
Faccenda Group Ltd
Greencore Group plc
Panesar Foods Ltd
Tulip Ltd
Health and Safety Laboratories
IOSH

Introduction

The Recipe for safety initiative

Recipe for safety is a joint initiative between the food and drink manufacturing industries and HSE to reduce injuries and ill health caused by work in those industries.

The initiative began in the early 1990s as a partnership between the Food and Drink Federation, trades unions and HSE's Food and Drink Manufacture section. In 2004, the initiative was expanded to include all the main food and drink trade associations and the Institution of Occupational Safety and Health (IOSH).

Over 20 years later the initiative continues to play an important and active part in improving health and safety in the food and drink industries and is currently overseen by the Food and Drink Manufacture Health and Safety Forum (see final section). Under the initiative, HSE and Forum member organisations:

- highlight the main health and safety issues in the industry and advise how to tackle them;
- regularly revise *A recipe for safety* to ensure guidance in this publication remains topical.

Success of the initiative

Since the Recipe for safety initiative began, the overall rate of injuries reportable to HSE has more than halved. There have also been considerable improvements in tackling ill health caused by work. However, the injury rate remains higher than Britain's 'all manufacture' average, allowing scope for further improvement.

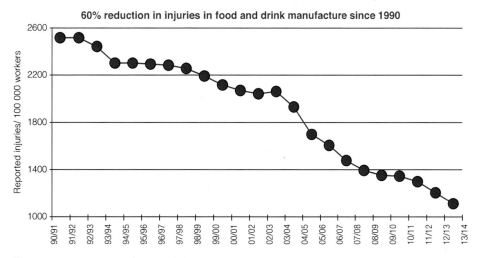

Figure 1 Injury rates in food and drink manufacture since 1990

Injury rates across the 30 food and drink manufacturing sectors (bakeries, meat processing, dairies etc) vary considerably, with some sectors well above the food and drink industries average and many well below. Even within these sectors injury rates and health and safety performance vary from company to company.

Please read on ... your involvement will benefit not only your company but the entire industry.

Summary

Key health and safety topics in the food and drink industries

Ninety-six per cent of all injuries and occupational ill health in food and drink manufacture are caused by the following:

- machinery
- workplace transport
- work at height
- entry into silos and confined spaces
- slips and trips
- struck by objects and knives
- manual handling
- upper limb disorders
- occupational dermatitis
- occupational asthma
- noise-induced hearing loss
- work-related stress

Managing these 12 key issues in your company will significantly reduce injuries, ill health and the associated costs.

You will need to take positive action to achieve continued improvement to health and safety performance. Concentrating on these key topics will maximise that improvement.

How to use this recipe

Use the information about injuries and ill health in this guidance

This guidance gives a wider perspective on the real risks in your sector of the food and drink industry and will help you set more realistic, quantified objectives for improvement. It will make you more aware of the need for positive action to improve both your own and the industry's overall injury and ill-health figures.

Concentrate on preventing the main causes of injuries and ill health

This guidance identifies the main priorities for each industry sector and outlines the key factors in making effective arrangements to prevent or protect against the risks caused by these priorities.

Review the effectiveness of your health and safety arrangements

Effective health and safety management is an essential part of running a business.

Guidance on reviewing your health and safety management and establishing effective arrangements to prevent or protect against the key health and safety risks is provided in 'Action plan for management'.

Key criteria for making significant performance improvements are:

- setting clear and realistic policy standards;
- the development and implementation of an easy-to-understand safety management system;
- communicating this information in a way that is easy to understand, even when translated.

The business benefits from avoiding accidents, ill health and accidental damage should help convince fellow managers. Health and safety arrangements need to be discussed with safety representatives or employee representatives – involvement at all levels is a key to success.

Why positive action is needed

HSE research indicates that positive steps by management could have prevented injury in about 70% of incidents, and action by workers a further 10%.

Effective management of work-related safety and health is good for business. Many companies have embedded this argument in the development of their health and safety policies and culture.

The added value comes from both ends of the balance sheet – reduced costs as well as higher efficiencies, productivity and profit. It is not just about the cost of claims and replacement labour, it is about the whole economic well-being of the business, as well as trust and reputation.

Ill health caused by work

Health is as important as safety. How people are cared for, whether at work or in the event of absence from whatever cause, is important to the business. There is potential for work in the food and drink industry to cause long-term ill health. However, as the effects are not always immediate, ill health may not get the same attention and allocation of resources as safety in delivering a long-term and sustainable benefit.

Supporting a timely return to work after absence is beneficial to both a company and its workers. But ill health in the workplace (and injuries which are not positively managed) can become chronic ill health and create incapacity in the future. Economic inactivity due to injury or ill health is not good for individuals or their employers.

Dealing positively with ill health caused or made worse by work is the critical factor in protecting the company and its workforce. A proactive occupational health team will deal with discomfort in the workplace before it becomes pain, sickness and absence. This will reduce the potential for incapacity arising from chronic ill health and reduce the risk of injury from accidents at the same time.

Effective management of health and safety makes good business sense

There are many reasons why, so please read on!

A number of major multi-site food and drink processing and distribution companies have assessed the full cost of accidents. This includes both the hidden and insured costs of all incidents. The results indicate that the true recoverable cost of accidents is an area that needs and justifies control. The same circumstances which caused injury also created production losses, quality and cost problems.

For many businesses, where margins are very tight, profits can depend on the control of costs – including loss from health and safety incidents – just as much as increased sales or higher prices.

The key to effective health and safety is strong leadership.

Human factors

Challenging attitudes and behaviours at all levels by encouraging safe behaviour and challenging unsafe behaviour can all be very effective in reducing injuries, ill health and other 'lost time' incidents. It requires leadership from the top, linked to engagement at all levels of the organisation.

In summary

Many companies in the food and drink industries get the most out of health and safety management programmes by applying the practices outlined in this 'recipe'. As a result, in addition to keeping their people healthy and safe, these companies see significant financial advantage and reduced risk to the business as a whole.

Following the guidance which follows makes good business sense!

Action plan for management

How to manage health and safety

Employers have a legal duty to put in place arrangements to manage health and safety.

Successful delivery can rarely be achieved by one-off interventions, a sustained and systematic approach may be necessary. This may not always require a formal health and safety management system, but whatever approach is used it probably contains the steps Plan, Do, Check, Act:

PLAN, DO, CHECK, ACT

- Plan
  - Determine your policy
  - Plan for implementation
- Do
  - Profile your organisation's health and safety risks
  - Organise for health and safety
  - Implement your plan
- Check
  - Measure performance
  - Investigate incidents
- Act
  - Review performance
  - Learn lessons

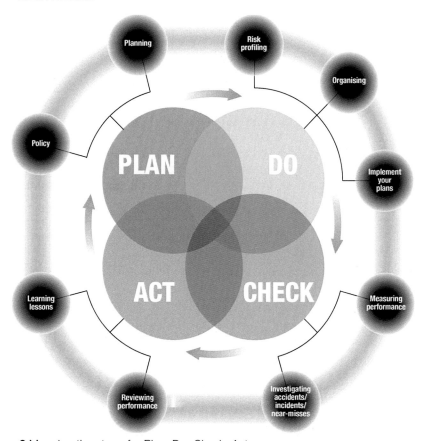

Figure 2 Mapping the steps for Plan, Do, Check, Act

Plan, Do, Check, Act should not be seen as a once-and-for-all action. You may need to go round the cycle more than once, particularly when:

● starting out;
● developing a new process, product or service;
● implementing any change.

Do you need a dedicated management system?

A formal management system can help and it's your decision whether to use a formal management system or framework. Examples include:

● national and international standards such as BS OHSAS 18001:2007 *Occupational health and safety management systems*;
● BS EN ISO 9001:2008 *Quality management system;*
● in-house standards, procedures or codes;
● sector-specific frameworks.

Although the language and methodology vary, the key actions usually relate to **Plan, Do, Check, Act.**

Consider the costs of getting it wrong

Health and safety failures can be costly.

Hidden costs may include:

● equipment or process damage / downtime;
● loss of production;
● absence of key workers due to injury or ill health;
● additional training costs;
● additional overtime;
● loss of reputation;
● management time and resources for investigation;
● increasing employers' liability insurance costs.

A large-scale incident such as fire and the damage it causes may result in your business being unable to run for a considerable period of time, the ramifications of which may be catastrophic for any business.

It's not just about production!

Consider other activities, not just production, when seeking to identify and control workplace risk, for example:

● cleaning activities – often involve different slip / trip and fall from height risks along with manual handling and health hazards. Additionally, factory hygiene teams often work at night with reduced levels of supervision and often need to intervene in machine operations, working with water, steam, hoses and other hazards;
● proactive and reactive maintenance activities – often require intrusive work involving removal of guarding systems, 'live working' to find faults, working at height, lone-working and out-of-hours work.

These issues will require specific safety controls, for example:

- isolation procedures for all forms of energy (including gas, electricity, hydraulics, high- and low-pressure air);
- provision of the most suitable access equipment for the task (such as scaffolding, tower scaffolds, mobile elevating work platforms (MEWPs));
- provision of adequate personal protective equipment (PPE) (such as eye protection that will not mist up).

Don't forget the HEALTH part of health and safety

All too often insufficient focus is given to ill health caused by work that can often lead to long-term or permanent damage. The main causes of occupational ill health in the food and drink industries include:

- musculoskeletal disorders (MSDs) – mainly comprising work-related upper limb disorders (ULDs) and back injuries;
- work-related stress – which can be caused by poor work organisation;
- asthma – for example from inhalation of flour and grain dusts;
- dermatitis – from hand washing, contact with foodstuffs, chemicals etc;
- noise-induced hearing loss – where noise levels exceed 80 decibels (dB).

How to manage work-related ill-health priorities

Companies should assess and manage health risks arising from work in the same way as safety risks. Health surveillance is not only needed for hazards which have workplace exposure limits (WELs) but also for other occupational health risks.

Examples of when health surveillance is likely to be required include where there is a risk of:

- occupational asthma (eg exposure to sensitisers such as grain dust, flour dust, fish or egg protein or spices);
- work-related ULDs;
- hearing loss from high noise levels;
- dermatitis or skin complaints from frequent hand washing or exposure to foods such as vegetable or fruit juices;
- ill health from work in hot or cold environments.

Remember: Some food materials may have a sensitising effect even at very low exposures.

The benefits of worker engagement

Engaging the workforce can lead to fewer injury and ill-health risks.

Consulting and involving safety representatives or employee representatives in planning, preparing systems of work, carrying out risk assessments and reviewing and discussing health and safety arrangements is essential.

Site management teams, safety representatives and others can often work together to proactively identify unsafe behaviours and their causes before an injury occurs – for example from poor equipment or workstation design, unrealistic production rates or inadequate training or supervision.

When considering how to involve the workforce, do not forget temporary or agency workers, migrant workers, visitors and contractors. Employers have an obligation to each and every one of them.

Human factors play an important part in avoiding accidents and ill health at work. Consequently, it is important to build human factors into risk assessments, procedures, training, assessing staffing and workload levels, safety-critical communications (eg shift handover), the design of control rooms and interfaces with machines.

Don't forget those whose first language is not English

There are many workers in the food and drink industries that do not speak or understand English. These workers may not readily understand instructions given to them, may be reluctant to admit they do not understand, or even – when they understand – do not interpret the information, instruction and training in the correct manner.

Focus on four main areas:

- **Training:** Individuals may be completely unfamiliar with workplace risks – make sure induction training is clear and simple.
- **Communication:** They may have problems communicating in English – make sure communications are clear and effective. Ensure workers understand what is required of them and know how to raise concerns if they are unsure.
- **Competence:** Before individuals start work, check that they have the qualifications or skills needed for the job.
- **Attitude to health and safety:** Make sure each individual understands the importance of health and safety in the workplace and how it is managed. Use effective supervision to identify and address any weaknesses in understanding training and instructions.

Solutions can include:

- translation of training materials and safe systems of work;
- training multilingual people in health, safety and training skills to allow them to deliver effective on-the-job training;
- using visual aids, posters;
- health and safety programmes to ensure all workers are able to consider the issues.

A checklist for improving your safety organisation

☐ **Cost** the full impact of accidents, work-related ill health and non-injury incidents on your business – measuring the full costs of losses can help convince everyone of the potential for cost savings to be made from good management of health and safety.

☐ **Calculate** your company's injury rate and compare it against your industry's benchmark.

☐ **Analyse** what type of incidents are occurring and look at your company's work-related ill-health absence. Then set quantified objectives, eg a specific reduction in a particular cause of injury.

☐ **Concentrate** your efforts and resources on the main causes of injury and ill health in conjunction with your assessment of what the main risks are in your company. In general, they are likely to be those highlighted in this guidance, but you may have some site-specific risks such as ammonia refrigeration or dust explosions. Start with the causes of injuries and illnesses that most damage quality of life. Give attention first to implementing the health and safety requirements which address these priorities and their underlying causes. Consult with those monitoring your workers' work-related ill health to identify where people are being harmed or affected by occupational factors.

☐ **Consider** the range of workers employed – age, language, cultural and educational backgrounds, gender issues (eg pregnancy, nursing mothers). Take these into account in risk assessments, planning and monitoring and associated communication.

☐ **Recognise** the need to have arrangements in place to control health and safety risks, including:

- a written health and safety policy (if you employ five or more people);
- assessments of the risks to employees, contractors, customers, partners, and any other people who could be affected by your activities. Record the significant findings in writing (if you employ five or more people). Any risk assessment must be 'suitable and sufficient';
- effective planning, organisation, control, monitoring and review of the preventive and protective measures that come from risk assessment;
- access to competent health and safety advice;
- providing employees with information about the risks in your workplace and how they are protected;
- instruction and training for employees in how to deal with the risks;
- adequate and appropriate supervision;
- consulting employees about their risks at work and current preventive and protective measures.

For advice and templates on these processes see HSE's risk management webpages for more information.

☐ **Consult** and involve safety representatives or employee representatives in planning, writing procedures, solving problems, reviewing and discussing health and safety arrangements.

☐ **Review** your written statement of policy, organisation and arrangements. Make sure people carry it out in practice and keep to it. Ensure it includes arrangements for tackling relevant priorities highlighted in this guidance.

The main causes of injuries by industry sector

Although the main causes of injuries are relevant across most food and drink industries, the following highlights those injuries most reported in different sectors:

grain... flour... animal feed
- handling and lifting – especially moving sacks
- falls from height – off ladders, stairs and vehicles
- slips and trips – more prominent than usual due to obstructions and uneven floors
- exposure to substances (eg chlorine, hydrochloric acid, sulphur dioxide)
- machinery – screw conveyors, rotary valves, roller mills, mixers (mostly during maintenance, cleaning, refilling etc)
- entry into silos – risk from engulfment, lack of a respirable atmosphere, mechanical hazards (eg sweep augers)
- transport – including lift trucks and trailers when tipping

bread... cakes... biscuits
- slips – mostly due to wet or contaminated floors
- handling and lifting – especially lifting and pushing / pulling heavy weights
- struck by an object (eg hand knife) or striking against an object
- machinery – conveyors, wrapping machinery, pie and tart machines, dough brakes, moulders, mixers, roll plant, pinning rolls / belts
- transport – including lift trucks

meat... poultry... fish... slaughtering
- being struck by an object – mostly by hand tools, including knives, especially during boning out
- handling and lifting – especially lifting heavy weights, pushing / pulling trolleys and contact with sharp edges
- slips – mostly on wet or greasy floors
- machinery – such as bandsaws, derinders, skinning machines, pie and tart machines, conveyors and packaging machinery
- transport – including lift trucks

milk... cheese
- handling and lifting – especially repetitive lifting, pushing / pulling heavy trolleys and contact with sharp edges
- slips – due to wet floors
- being struck by an object – mostly falling objects, sometimes hand tools
- exposure to substances – cleaning fluids, splashes, CIP (clean-in-place) failures, steam, hot water, chemical fume
- falls from height – off ladders, stairs, tanks and from vehicles / tankers
- transport – including tanker movements and lift trucks
- machinery – lifting machines, conveyors, packaging machines

fruit... vegetables
- handling and lifting – especially repetitive lifting and moving boxes etc
- contact with sharp edges
- slips – due to wet floors
- being struck by an object – mostly falling packages, sometimes hand tools
- falls from height – off ladders, work platforms, stairs and from vehicles
- striking against fixed or movable objects
- machinery – conveyors, packaging machines, slicing machines, palletisers
- transport – including lift trucks

chocolate... sugar confectionery
- handling and lifting – especially repetitive lifting, pushing / pulling heavy loads or contact with sharp edges
- slips – due to wet / contaminated floors
- being struck by an object – mostly falling packages, sometimes hand tools
- striking against fixed or movable objects
- machinery – conveyors, packaging machines
- exposure to harmful substances – burns and scalds from carrying open containers of hot product, manual dispensing of caustic cleaners

beer... spirits... soft drinks
- handling and lifting – especially barrels, casks and drink packs
- slips – mostly due to wet floors
- being struck by falling objects – barrels, casks, drink packs
- falls from height – off ladders, work platforms, stairs and from vehicles
- machinery – conveyors, bottling machines, packaging machines, palletisers
- exposure to harmful substances – cleaning chemicals, hot liquids
- transport – especially lift trucks

Further guidance

See HSE webpages on:

Managing for health and safety www.hse.gov.uk/managing/index.htm
Risk management www.hse.gov.uk/risk/index.htm
Human factors www.hse.gov.uk/humanfactors/index.htm
Migrant workers www.hse.gov.uk/migrantworkers/index.htm
Food and drink manufacture www.hse.gov.uk/food/index.htm
Consulting and involving your workers www.hse.gov.uk/involvement/index.htm
Leadership www.hse.gov.uk/leadership/
Competence www.hse.gov.uk/competence/

Also

Health and Safety at Work etc Act 1974 is at www.hse.gov.uk/legislation/hswa.htm

Health and safety priorities and their management

Machinery

Why workplace machinery is a priority

Machinery and plant accounts for a third of all fatalities in the food and drink industries, making it the highest cause of fatalities. Machinery also accounts for a significant proportion of non-fatal injuries – in 75% of cases there was no or inadequate guarding and in 25% of cases cleaning was taking place.

The law

The Provision and Use of Work Equipment Regulations 1998 (PUWER) require:

- selection and provision of suitable work equipment;
- safeguarding of machinery and equipment;
- maintenance and inspection of machinery and equipment, including safety checks on fixed and movable guards, interlock switches etc;
- training on how to use machines, how to deal with process problems etc;
- clearly labelled and accessible controls, including emergency stop devices and means for isolation / disconnection.

If a machine is dangerous (eg you can reach dangerous parts when dealing with a process problem, removing product, cleaning etc) then you need to look again at the safeguarding options.

How to manage the risks of working with new and existing machinery

Existing machinery
Machinery requires regular examination to ensure it is safe. Over time the needs of the business change and the uses of machines change and develop, as do the practices involved in running and maintaining them. When inspecting machines, guards and other safety features, make sure that consideration is given to:

- when the machine is running normally;
- when it is being cleaned;
- start-up procedure, film / reel changing etc;
- when it is being repaired / inspected / adjusted;
- when jams are being cleared.

It is especially important in the food and drink industries to remember that the operator needs frequent, easy access to:

- assist product flow;
- clear blockages;
- allow changeover of product types;
- clean the machinery.

Fixed guards (ie requiring a hand tool to remove them) are in many cases unsuitable. Hinged guards are often preferable, with a high standard of interlocks, eg coded magnetic interlocks. The effectiveness of safety controls depends on many factors, including the operator's method of work and the demands of the task.

If during routine examinations it is discovered that guards are being removed, safety interlocks defeated etc ask **why**. This may highlight a process problem which needs to be fixed and which is being hidden by the adoption of unauthorised procedures.

New machinery

When purchasing new equipment, seek to adopt high safety standards at the outset by using informed purchasing procedures. These should ensure the correct specification, selection and checking of new equipment and involve operators and engineers with experience in the types of equipment being purchased.

All new machinery should be:

- safe: that means provided with all necessary guards and protective devices;
- CE-marked (CE marking is not a guarantee that the machinery is safe, only the manufacturer's claim that the product meets all relevant supply EC Directive requirements);
- provided with an EC Declaration of Conformity (ask for a copy if you have not been given one);
- provided with instructions in English. These instructions should state:
  - how to assemble, install, use, adjust and maintain the machinery, including dealing with blockages and, where processing foodstuffs, for hygienic cleaning;
  - details on the protective measures to take, such as when PPE should be provided and used;
  - warnings of ways in which machinery must not be used;
  - any remaining residual risks that need to be controlled by safe systems of work.

Machinery must be built to the appropriate European Standards (BS EN Standards) for that type of machine or equipment, or in direct conformity with the Essential Health and Safety Requirements (EHSRs) of the Machinery Directive (2006/42/EC).

Even if your machines are CE-marked, when internally assessing the effectiveness of the safeguards, remember to:

- give consideration to your previous accident or near-miss reports which may have exposed failings;
- learn from other businesses within your industry – often learning from others' investigations can be helpful in improving your own methods and controls.

Conveyors

Conveyors are involved in 30% of all machinery accidents in the food and drink industries – more than any other class of machine. In particular:

- 90% of conveyor injuries occur on flat-belt conveyors;
- 90% of the injuries involve well-known hazards such as in-running nips between the belt and end roller, transmission parts and trapping points between moving and fixed parts;
- 90% of accidents occur during normal foreseeable operations – production activities, clearing blockages, cleaning etc.

Safeguarding hazardous parts of conveyors may be achieved by:

- design (eg lift-out rollers that prevent finger trapping);
- fixed guarding (requiring a hand tool such as a spanner to remove) where daily or frequent cleaning is not required;
- hinged or removable interlocked guards (eg guards fitted with coded, magnetic interlock switches to prevent the machine running with the guard removed).

A safe system of work should be in place for daily and routine cleaning of conveyors that ensures workers are not placed at risk of injury from unguarded moving parts. The system of work used should be monitored and workers appropriately trained.

Case studies

Case study 1
An engineer suffered fatal crushing injuries when working within the danger area of a large robotic palletising machine. The machine started up unexpectedly as it had not been electrically isolated and the power locked off. In food and drink manufacturing, around one fatality a year results from workers entering large machines which have not been safely isolated and locked off from electric, hydraulic or pneumatic power sources. Systems should be in place to ensure workers entering machines are safe, for example by locking off the power source and the worker taking the key with them into the machine.

Case study 2
A worker cleaning underneath one end of a conveyor belt in a packing area had his hand and arm drawn into the running nip between the belt and the end roller. His injuries included loss of the arm. The guarding had been removed without the conveyor being electrically isolated.

Case study 3
A maintenance fitter was injured by a chain and sprocket transmission drive when he was greasing part of a cake line in a cake factory which had a history of similar accidents. HSE served an Improvement Notice on the company requiring a review of routine maintenance for all plant and equipment. The review identified the access hazards and devised safeguards so these activities could be carried out safely. The company substantially re-guarded much of their plant, allowing maintenance operations to take place safely. They reinforced this work with awareness training and set up safe systems of work for maintenance personnel.

Further guidance

See HSE webpages on:

Work equipment and machinery
www.hse.gov.uk/work-equipment-machinery/index.htm
Food processing machinery www.hse.gov.uk/food/machinery.htm
Packaging machinery www.hse.gov.uk/food/package.htm

Also

Buying new machinery: A short guide to the law and your responsibilities when buying new machinery for use at work INDG271 HSE Books 2011
www.hse.gov.uk/pubns/indg271.htm

Workplace transport

Why workplace transport is a priority

Workplace transport accounts for a quarter of on-site fatalities in the food and drink industries. Where there is movement of people and vehicles together there is a high risk of accidents and serious injury occurring. More so when sites work around the clock and in all weather conditions.

In addition to injuries resulting directly from the vehicle, other related injuries can arise – for example as a result of falling from a vehicle or being struck by pallet handlers, trolleys etc.

How to manage the risks of workplace transport

The key is to assess risk against each of the three main factors:

- driver
- vehicle
- site

Driver
Consider the following:

- medical fitness to drive;
- training and an appropriate vehicle licence;
- whether the driver understands the risks and safe systems of work;
- competency assessments for drivers with mechanisms for review;
- driver fatigue management (linked with driving hours);
- how agency drivers are inducted and trained;
- managing drivers from foreign countries (eg clear visual instructions);
- reversing instructions and use of visual aids, including mirrors;
- safe use of manual handling equipment in and out of vehicles, eg pump trucks.

Vehicle
Consider the following:

- selection of vehicle for the task;
- suitable seat restraints and driver protection (eg rollover protective structures and falling object protective structures);
- maintenance of vehicle and checking of tail lifts by a competent body;
- loads being properly secured (Note: Curtains on vehicles are not load restraints);
- adequate mirrors and reversing aids (eg audible device to warn pedestrians, cameras etc);
- where possible, avoid work on top of vehicles; have controls at ground level;
- safe use of tail lifts;
- earthing of vehicles when unloading materials which could ignite.

Site
Consider the following:

- clearly mark vehicle routes on site – (eg use site maps, stopping point instructions and one-way systems);
- segregate people and vehicles;
- measures to reduce speed (eg speed limits and speed humps);
- where possible, avoid reversing – check there are warning systems for reversing and use trained banksmen in high-risk areas as a last resort;

- adequate lighting levels;
- procedures for poor weather conditions (eg snow / ice);
- determining blind spots for drivers; use blind spot mirrors or similar;
- maintain good surface conditions;
- prevent drive-aways at loading docks, eg use of ignition key control, traffic lights, captive keys and interlocks linked to bay doors;
- mark vehicle loading and unloading areas with vehicle stops to avoid property damage, for example when reversing;
- safe working at height (eg from tail lifts);
- for off-site delivery points consider delivery point risks, which include access / egress, lighting, pedestrians and loading / unloading controls.

Additional transport risks relevant to the food and drink industries

Some key facts:

- Lift trucks are a particular hazard in the workplace
- Lift trucks are involved in 24% of all workplace transport accidents
- Accidents involving lift trucks are often due to poor supervision and a lack of training

Fork lift trucks (FLTs) – lifting people

People should never be lifted on the forks or on a pallet, or similar, mounted on the forks because they can easily fall off – this has led to many fatalities and serious injuries.

However, in certain circumstances where the work has been planned, FLTs can be used with an integrated working platform to allow people to work at height. Integrated working platforms are cage attachments with controls that are linked to and isolate the truck controls so that only a person on the platform can control the height of the platform and truck movements.

FLTs – loading / unloading

FLTs falling from loading bays: Injuries to FLT drivers occur when the FLT falls down the gap between the loading bay and lorry when the lorry unexpectedly drives off. Consider safeguards such as holding the driver's keys until the lorry / trailer doors are locked closed, or a solid restraint attaching the rear of the lorry to the loading bay with a captive key linked to the bay doors.

FLTs on articulated trailers: Uncoupled trailers can tip when the FLT moves forward of the trailer legs, leading to accidents. Also consider if the strength of the trailer floor is sufficient for a loaded FLT.

Tipping lorries

Overturning of tipping lorries and trailers: Tipping lorries and trailers can overturn when raised to discharge their load. Consider alternative non-tipping vehicle options, stabilisers or air suspension dumping during tipping, level and stable ground, driver training for viscous and sticking loads and training drivers not to jump out of a toppling vehicle.

Tailgate safety on bulk delivery vehicles: Deaths have occurred when a slug of viscous material slides down a raised trailer and throws open the latched or unlatched tailgate, hitting the driver. Drivers should be instructed to stand clear of tailgate and vibratory equipment. Also, practise dust control by fitting a sock to the grain hatch or dust extraction at bunded hoppers.

Tail lifts

Safety in the use of tail lifts: Hands and feet can get trapped during raising / lowering of the tail lift – where possible, design out trapping points. Ensure training is given in the safe operation of tail lifts. Consider precautions (such as raised edges) to prevent roll cages falling from raised tail lifts.

Trailers and tractor units

Coupling and uncoupling: Vehicle 'runaways' can occur during the uncoupling of trailers from tractor units. When coupling or uncoupling hoses, drivers should always turn off the engine, ensure the parking brakes on both the tractor unit and trailer are applied and, where possible, remove the keys.
Drivers should never rely on disconnecting the red supply airline ('dropping the red line') as a way of applying the parking brake. They should always apply the trailer parking brake using the control button on the trailer. There is no exclusion from these requirements for shunting operations.

Case studies

Case study 1
An HGV driver saw his vehicle move away when no brakes had been applied. The driver was crushed between his vehicle and another vehicle as he ran to stop it and died as a result.

Case study 2
A pallet loaded with flour fell from a lorry being unloaded by a lorry-mounted crane. An employee was trapped by the legs and died two weeks later in hospital.

Case study 3
A dispatch clerk employee wearing a high-visibility jacket was killed crossing a large open warehouse when she was struck by a loading shovel which entered the warehouse via a side entrance.

Case study 4
An agency lorry driver on site was unloading empty bread baskets. His head became caught in the tail lift mechanism and he died as a result.

Further guidance

See HSE webpages on:

Vehicles at work www.hse.gov.uk/workplacetransport/index.htm

Work at height

Why work at height is a priority

Controlling risk from working at height is an important priority because falls from height are the third highest cause of fatal injury in the food and drink industries, comprising 20% of fatal accidents.

Falls from height also result in around 80 major injuries (broken limbs, fractured skulls etc) each year, as well as a further 230 over-3-day absence injuries.

The law

The Work at Height Regulations 2005 provide a practical framework for managing the risk. Where work at height cannot be avoided a series of actions should be taken to control the risk. The hierarchy of control requires practical measures to prevent a fall, such as handrails and MEWPs, before considering fall restraint and arrest equipment.

Where access is required to a high level on a regular basis for routine tasks, permanent safe means of access should be provided. The schedules to the Regulations set out specific requirements for access equipment. Providing fixed stairways and platforms with appropriate handrails, guard rails and toe boards is part of the overhead cost of providing work equipment.

Where work at height takes place in non-routine or infrequent circumstances, a temporary means of access will need to be provided. This includes portable ladders, stepladders, scaffolds, portable towers and various forms of MEWPs.

Protective measures must be selected to control risk 'so far as is reasonably practicable' or SFAIRP. Selection needs to reflect proper and careful consideration of risk – balancing cost and delay against the worst case risk of injury.

How to manage the risks of work at height

Places and activities giving rise to falls
Working at height is required in a wide range of activities including:

- manufacturing and processing operations;
- cleaning and hygiene activities;
- maintenance and engineering work;
- on vehicles and loading bays;
- ancillary activities in stores, workshops and service areas.

An analysis of fall accidents
Analysis of three years' food and drink industry data reported to HSE highlights the places / equipment from where workers fell:

- ladders: 40%
- vehicles / FLTs (see below): 17%
- machinery / plant: 10%
- platforms: 10%
- stairs: 8%
- roof / false ceiling: 7%
- scaffold / gantry: 4%
- warehouse racking: 4%

Where vehicles were involved:

- 35% fell from a lorry
- 31% fell from FLT forks
- 13% from cab steps
- 9% from top of a vehicle
- 4% from tanker steps

The same analysis highlighted the activity being undertaken at the time of the fall:

- Cleaning or maintenance was usually being undertaken where falls were from scaffolding / gantries, ladders, roofs or through false ceilings.
- Where falls were from vehicles, the activity being carried out was usually part of the normal loading / unloading procedure. The main exception was falls from FLT forks where workers were either standing on the forks or on a pallet mounted on the forks in order to gain access to high areas, eg to change light fittings or maintain / clean plant.
- Where the fall was from machinery / plant, in a third of cases cleaning was being carried out, in a third of cases checking or sampling was being carried out, and in a third of cases maintenance was being carried out.
- Falls from storage racking occurred when workers were retrieving stored goods at high level by climbing up the racking – rather than using wheeled steps or similar, which were usually provided.

What you need to do

- Avoid work at height if you can

- Where it is not possible to avoid work at height use work equipment to prevent falls

- Where it is not possible to eliminate the risk of a fall use work equipment or other measures to minimise the distance and consequences of a fall, should one occur

Figure 3 Work at height – fall prevention hierarchy

Internal ceilings

Internal ceilings formed when food rooms are constructed from laminated panels can be too fragile to walk on.

Where access onto these ceilings is required, for example for plant maintenance or access to services such as ammonia lines, it is necessary to ensure any risk of falling through the ceiling is assessed and preventative measures implemented.

Figure 4 Fixed access system integral to new plant

Where frequent access is required, permanent walkways with handrails should be provided. The walkways must be capable of taking the weight of workers, their toolboxes and any plant or equipment to be carried.

Where access is infrequent, an assessment should be carried out to determine the precautions required, taking into account the loads mentioned above.

Figure 5 Fragile internal ceiling

Roof work

Roof work is a particularly high-risk activity. Access to external roofs may be required for:

- maintenance (eg clearing gutters or repairing leaks);
- servicing rooftop plant rooms, oven and fryer flues, ventilation systems, explosion vents, coolers, fans and trunking;
- pest control purposes (roof areas are prone to infestation or providing a route of entry to the factory for various insect, rodent and bird pests).

Risks include:

- falls from the roof edge;
- falls through fragile or slippery roof materials and skylights;
- exposure to inclement weather conditions which might amplify any risk;
- lone working.

Where roof access is required on a regular basis, the following should be provided:

- permanent safe means of access to working areas;
- a system to prevent unauthorised access onto the roof;
- roof edge protection and fragile material edge protection;
- safe crawling / walking boards and fallboards on fragile roof areas where access is required;
- anchor points and/or cables – might be needed to facilitate use of harnesses with fall restraint or arrest equipment where fixed systems cannot be installed.

Figure 6 Walkway and fallboards on fragile roof

Figure 7 Skylight and roof edge protection

A checklist for managing work at height

- Can the work be done without working at height?
- Can the work be carried out from an existing safe place of work?
- Where work at height cannot be avoided:
  - has a suitable and sufficient risk assessment been completed for work at height?
  - are appropriate risk control measures in place?
  - have findings of the assessment been communicated to relevant staff and are they suitably trained and competent?
  - is the assessment reviewed from time to time, and whenever conditions and/or the work or specific tasks change?
- Are permanent fixed access and fall prevention systems fit for purpose and properly inspected and maintained?
- Are portable / temporary / mobile access systems (including harnesses, lines and fixing points):
  - inspected, tested and maintained in accordance with the Work at Height Regulations (regulation 12), PUWER (Provision and Use of Work Equipment Regulations) and LOLER (Lifting Equipment and Lifting Operations Regulations)?
  - fit for purpose and suitable for the requirements of the task, eg a ladder might be suitable for inspecting an overhead conveyor, but a higher standard of access equipment such as a MEWP may be required for maintenance work on the conveyor?
  - listed in a 'register' and tagged or labelled with identifying marks to enable control over (and recording of) use, inspection and maintenance?
  - constructed and inspected by competent people?
  - for scaffolds – inspected before first use / every seven days and after inclement weather or change?
- Are 'safe systems of work' and, if relevant, permits, used for tasks where significant risk remains?
- Are all staff who need to be, fit for work at height tasks?
- Is work at height adequately supervised?
- Is appropriate signage and labelling used and maintained in conjunction with access systems and equipment?
- Is all this applied to contractors?

Case studies

Case study 1
A food industry factory worker fell through a skylight when he accompanied a pest control contractor on a visit to a factory roof. The worker sat on a skylight made of fragile material. It gave way and the worker fell 8 m to a concrete factory floor. He survived life-threatening leg and head injuries but will never fully recover. The site had invested in fixed access systems, roof edge protection and a safe system of work, but consideration had not been given to the fragile material of the skylight.

Case study 2
Even falls from a minimal height can cause high severity injury. An engineer in a bakery attending a fault on a cooler stepped back and fell backwards off the concrete mounting plinth of the cooler 500 mm to the bakery floor. He struck his head and suffered fatal injuries.

Further guidance

See HSE webpages on:

Falls from height www.hse.gov.uk/falls/index.htm
Food manufacture falls from height www.hse.gov.uk/food/falls.htm
Falls from vehicles www.hse.gov.uk/fallsfromvehicles/workers.htm

Also

Working at height: A brief guide INDG401 HSE Books 2014
www.hse.gov.uk/pubns/indg401.pdf

Entry into silos and confined spaces

Why entry into silos and confined spaces is a priority

Workers and rescue workers without proper training are killed every year when they fail to take adequate safeguards to protect themselves before entering a confined space. The dangers of working in confined spaces are well known; even so, fatal accidents still occur.

How to manage the risks of entry into silos and confined spaces

What is a confined space?
A confined space is a place which is substantially enclosed (though not always entirely) and where serious injury can occur from hazardous substances or conditions within the space.

Examples of confined spaces include tanks, reaction vessels, effluent pits, drains and silos where there may be lack of oxygen, an engulfment risk from grain, liquids etc or the presence of gases such as carbon dioxide or argon.

Rooms may become confined spaces if sealed to reduce dust or noise during maintenance.

Some gases are heavier than air and some are odourless and can only be detected by monitoring equipment.

Designing out the need to enter confined spaces
Design out the need to enter confined spaces. For example:

- design or modify silos and vessels so they are self-cleaning and material runs freely;
- if necessary, fit vibration pads, other flow aids or CIP systems;
- use remotely-operated silo cleaning and unblocking equipment so that entry is unnecessary if bridging or blocking occurs;
- confined spaces can often be cleaned from outside using modified tools, pressure lances etc;
- equipment such as sump pumps can often be located outside the confined space preventing the need for entry;
- use remote cameras for internal inspection of vessels.

Before people are asked to work in any confined space, decide if it is absolutely necessary or whether the work can be completed in some other way.

A checklist for a safe system of working within confined spaces

Where avoidance of entry into confined spaces is not reasonably practicable, make sure there is a safe system for working inside the space before entry. Identify the necessary precautions to reduce the risk of injury and ensure everyone involved is properly trained and instructed in what to do. The following checklist covers the essential elements in a safe system of work and the main safety issues to consider:

- Appoint a suitably trained supervisor to plan and check safety.
- People entering confined spaces should have sufficient training and experience.
- Ensure isolation of all services (electrical, mechanical, water, steam, ingredients etc) and prevention of any other forms of danger (product fall etc).
- Clean the confined space before entry to remove residues.
- Prevent entry into silos which still contain enough material to pose an engulfment / asphyxiation risk from becoming trapped by moving product such as grain, flour or sugar.
- Check the size of the entrance to ensure it is big enough to allow worker entry with all the necessary equipment and will provide ready access and egress in an emergency.
- Provide suitable ventilation by increasing the number of openings to improve ventilation or by providing forced ventilation. (Warning: Carbon monoxide in the exhaust from petrol-fuelled engines is so dangerous that use of such equipment in confined spaces should never be allowed.)
- Test the atmosphere in vessels and silos before entry and while inside. Check for noxious fumes or gases and measure oxygen levels using calibrated equipment. A confined space may have either too little or too much oxygen, both of which are dangerous. If it is not possible to clear the atmosphere or the atmosphere is oxygen-deficient use suitable breathing apparatus.
- Canister or cartridge respirators will not be suitable for most confined space work as they do not protect against high concentrations of gases or oxygen deficiency.
- Provide non-sparking tools and specially protected lighting if flammable or potentially explosive atmospheres are likely.
- Emergency procedures are vital – produce them and practise them. In particular, practise procedures to get people out in an emergency.
- Provide rescue harnesses – these should run back to a point outside the confined space.
- Communications should be good between inside and outside the confined space.
- Check how the alarm will be raised. Is it necessary to have someone outside the confined space to keep watch and communicate with those inside, to raise the alarm and take charge of the rescue procedure?
- Is a permit-to-work necessary? This ensures a formal check is undertaken to ensure all the elements of a safe system of work are in place before work is started in the confined space.

Remember always

- Conduct an adequate and sufficient risk assessment.
- Devise a safe system of work and provide the necessary equipment and training.
- Ensure trained emergency back-up as many fatalities are of rescuers entering to rescue the initial victim.
- Maintain a register of all confined spaces identified within the business, paying particular attention to those confined spaces away from the main operational areas.

Case studies

Case study 1

Over a number of years, crystallised sugar had stuck to the walls of a silo, reducing its capacity. Workers were sent inside to remove the sugar from the silo walls. Larger than anticipated quantities fell off the sides and buried them. One worker was killed instantly. Rescue was difficult because the silo could only be entered at the top.

Case study 2

A worker was preparing to clean a beverage storage tank. The tank had been previously cleaned and purged with nitrogen gas. The worker crawled through a small manhole to position the spray ball in the centre of the tank in order to spray the inside walls with detergent. After approximately five minutes in the tank, he was found unconscious and could not be revived. The nitrogen, an inert gas, had displaced the oxygen inside the tank and there was not enough oxygen to sustain life. The air in the tank was not tested for oxygen content before entry.

Case study 3

Effluent pits, balancing tanks and sewers can present a significant risk. For example, gas from rotting vegetation presents a significant risk to safety. It can produce hydrogen sulphide with the distinctive aroma of rotting eggs. This is both flammable and harmful. Good entry procedures are required supported by ongoing monitoring and effective emergency / rescue procedures.

> **Case study 4**
> Two maintenance workers were asked to inspect and repair the pumps in an old mild steel water buffering tank. Access to the confined space was top entry, via a ladder. The tank had been emptied, isolated and locked off. About 8 cm of water
> remained in the tank, resulting in heavy corrosion which affected the oxygen level; this should have been 20.9% and it was in fact 4%. The employees only entered the tank after carrying out pre-entry checks and then selecting and using the appropriate equipment. This prevented a fatality.

Further guidance

See HSE webpages on:

Confined spaces www.hse.gov.uk/confinedspace/index.htm

Also

Safe work in confined spaces: Confined Spaces Regulations 1997: Approved Code of Practice, Regulations and guidance L101 HSE Books 2009
www.hse.gov.uk/pubns/books/l101.htm

Slips and trips

Why slips and trips are a priority

Slip and trip injuries in the food and drink industries:

● result from slips (75%) and trips (25%), often arising from poorly managed work areas;
● comprise over a third of the major injuries (broken bones, hospitalisation etc) reported to HSE and over a quarter of injuries result in several days or more off work;
● can be serious, painful and debilitating – around 95% of the major injuries arising from slips and trips result in broken bones, cracked ribs, fractured skulls, dislocated shoulders etc;
● can very often be serious or even fatal – for example a fall from height or a fall into a machine.

How to manage the risks of slips and trips

A common misconception is that injuries caused by slips just happen and that little can be done to prevent them. This is not true – they can be managed and significantly reduced. Studies show that the biggest barriers to taking action are:

● not taking the injury risks seriously (or appreciating the injury costs involved);
● not understanding the causes of slipping (ie thinking that slips are inevitable);
● poor management controls.

Slip prevention can be managed very effectively and can cut serious injuries by 50% or more, significantly reducing costs and lost time.

Assessment of risk – the slip / trip potential model
For the most part, the slip / trip risk factors illustrated in Figure 8 are quite straightforward and do not require special skills or knowledge. Each potential risk factor is considered separately, below.

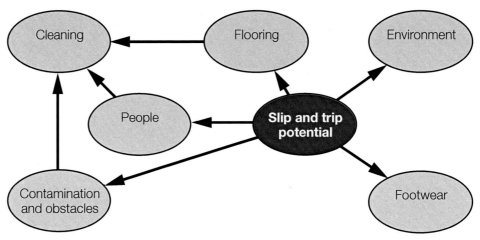

Figure 8 The main factors contributing to pedestrian slip and trip risks

Flooring

Slip resistance: Floors which are likely to get wet, greasy or be subjected to spillages should be slip resistant.

Slip resistance is dependent on the correct surface roughness (www.hse.gov.uk/ slips/sat/faqsurf.htm) (this roughness is microscopic). The micro-roughness required depends on the likely source of contamination – the thicker the contaminant, the higher the level of surface micro-roughness required. For example, this is the surface roughness required for the following sources of contamination:

- water – at least 20 microns
- milk – at least 45 microns
- stock – at least 60 microns
- cooking oil – at least 70 microns

Using the pendulum test for slip resistance: A test for floor slip resistance is the pendulum test – manufacturers give results of this test as 'pendulum test value' (PTV). Check results for the right conditions; most floors will have a good PTV when clean and dry but, if the floor is likely to get wet, the 'dry' PTV result will be irrelevant.

Laying new floors: When laying new floors, ensure that the laid floor actually matches the designed slip resistance, as a poorly laid floor may not match its specification. A good floor needs to be properly laid.

Maintaining existing floors and walkways: HSE's downloadable slips assessment tool (SAT) (www.hse.gov.uk/slips/sat/index.htm) software is a very useful tool that allows the operator to assess the slip potential of pedestrian walkway surfaces. Also, consider the following questions:

- Can you improve existing floors with anti-slip treatment (acid etching etc) and anti-slip stair nosings?

- Are you using the correct cleaning method and cleaning materials to maintain slip resistance?
- Do you check for loose, damaged and worn flooring and replace as needed?
- Is adequate floor drainage provided and is it in the right location?
- Are you making sure slopes or steps are clearly visible and marked where necessary, eg with anti-slip marker tapes and paints?
- Do you keep walkways free from obstructions at all times?

Footwear

Where floors cannot be kept clean and dry, slip-resistant footwear (www.hse.gov.uk/slips/footprocure.htm) is readily available and can prevent slip accidents. Be sure to:

- trial footwear first to make sure it is suitable for the environment and those who will be wearing it (ie comfort and fit);
- involve your staff in footwear selection.

Cleaning

Poor cleaning methods can lead to floors remaining slippery. Ensure the cleaning method (www.hse.gov.uk/pubns/web/slips02.pdf) is effective for the type and specification of floor in use and make effective arrangements for both routine cleaning and dealing with spills. In all cases:

- use the appropriate detergent at the correct concentration;
- remember the contact time of detergent is critically important;
- leave smooth floors dry after cleaning or exclude pedestrians until floor is dry;
- remove spillages promptly;
- do not introduce more slip or trip risks while cleaning, eg excess cleaning agent or trailing cables.

Contamination

Floors should always be dry (90% of slips occur on wet floors) and free from food and liquid contamination. Control the risks by:

- effective use of entrance matting;
- fixing leaks from machinery, plant, equipment, roofs etc immediately;
- designing tasks to minimise spillages;
- planning pedestrian and vehicle routes to avoid contaminated areas.

Environment

Ensure good lighting, even surfaces and lack of obstacles.

People or human factors

How people act and behave in their work environment can affect slips and trips. Control the risks by:

- dealing with spillages instead of waiting for someone else to deal with them;
- wearing slip-resistant footwear;
- avoiding rushing, carrying large objects that obscure vision or being distracted, eg by using a mobile phone.

A checklist for managing slips prevention

Arrangements to manage slips prevention include:

- assessment of the causes of slips and whether these are controlled – remember to include seasonal and climatic factors;
- elimination of sources of wet (or other) contamination of floors, walkways, staircases, gantries etc.

If a risk remains:

- set up a managed and effective cleaning regime;
- use the appropriate detergent, mixed at the right concentration for the correct contact time;
- two-stage mopping is key (using a wet mop, then a dry mop to remove water);
- clear up contamination and dry floors effectively as soon as possible;
- provide suitable floors with adequate drainage;
- provide adequate marking and lighting;
- trial footwear in your workplace before buying to make sure it is suitable for your floors, and comfortable;
- train staff and ensure tasks do not require them to move or carry goods inappropriately in a residually slippery area.

A checklist for managing trips prevention

Other causes of falling on the level are trips. Trips prevention is related to housekeeping management and effective solutions are often very simple, low cost and easy to implement. For example:

- Floors or the surface of the traffic route should be suitable, in good condition and kept free from obstructions.
- Floors should be free from holes, unevenness or slopes which expose any person to a risk to their safety.
- People must be able to move around safely.
- A system for removal of materials or objects likely to cause tripping is key.

Case studies

Case study 1
An employee was injured when walking past a tray area in a large bakery. The floor was wet from run-off and from pre-wash spray. The man, who was wearing normal outdoor shoes, slipped and fell, breaking his femur. A non-slip surface was subsequently installed and the control of water spray was implemented. Additionally, suitable safety footwear was issued with soles that provided better grip in wet conditions.

Case study 2
In a plant bakery a worker slipped in a puddle of fat on the floor at the corner of a fryer. Her arm went into the reservoir of hot fat in the fryer causing bums to her arm and hand. The fat was leaking from a faulty valve. The valve was replaced and a system set up to spot and clean up spills.

For more case studies see www.hse.gov.uk/slips/experience.htm.

Further guidance

See HSE webpages on:

Slips www.hse.gov.uk/slips/index.htm
Slips Assessment Tool (SAT) www.hse.gov.uk/slips/sat/index.htm
Flooring Selection Tool www.hse.gov.uk/slips/flooring-selection-tool.htm
Assessing the slip resistance of flooring www.hse.gov.uk/pubns/geis2.htm

Also

HSE's online learning tool – *Slips and Trips eLearning Package 'STEP'* is at www.hse.gov.uk/slips/step/start.htm

Struck by objects and knives

Why 'struck by' incidents with objects and knives is a priority

Being struck by moving or falling objects, or being struck by hand tools (especially knives), is common in the food and drink industries.

'Struck by' injuries cause around 15% of reportable injuries, some of which are fatal.

How to manage the risks of being struck by objects and knives

Internal product movement
Unlike product which is shrink-wrapped to secure it on the pallet prior to dispatch, loads being moved within the factory by pump trucks and lift trucks are often not properly secured.

Unsecured loads falling off pallets while being moved around the factory is a common cause of 'struck by' accidents. Pre-wrapping loads and having wide and unobstructed access routes will help minimise the risk.

Falling objects
Keep pedestrians away from pallet racking areas when lift trucks are in operation, as it is not uncommon for loads to fall from pallets as they are being lifted onto or retrieved from racking.

Pedestrians (including drivers) should be kept away from lorry loading / unloading operations in case a load falls. Note also that where curtain sided lorries have bulging sides, indicating load shift during transit, a safe method of work must be devised before unloading starts to ensure the load does not fall while the straps are being undone.

Flying objects
Although not a cause of many reportable injuries, in many food and drink factories minor injuries are caused by ingredients getting into eyes. Looking at your operations and reviewing past incidents may tell you whether eye protection should be used in specific processes.

Knife injuries
Operatives who use knives should receive relevant training in the safe issue, use, carrying, storage, cleaning, sharpening and disposal of knives.

Keeping knives sharp is important as it means less force is required for the task and, consequently, the operator will tend to have greater control. Note, however, that knives should not be sharpened so much that the blade becomes very thin, as this increases the risk of puncture wounds. A template can be used for knives to indicate when a blade has worn too thin for safe use.

Suitable PPE for knife use
Cut-resistant gloves should be used for the non-knife hand, but not all cut-resistant gloves offer the same level of protection. European Standard BS EN388 *Protective*

gloves against mechanical risks specifies five levels of protection (1–5), the higher number giving a greater level of protection.

There is usually a trade-off between dexterity and the level of protection, but aim to get the highest level of protection consistent with getting the job done. For the highest risk work, chainmail gloves and possibly wrist guards may be necessary to give adequate protection.

For work that involves pulling the knife back towards the body, such as some deboning tasks, then chainmail aprons should be worn.

Figure 9 Protective clothing for meat cutting

Case studies

Case study 1
A maintenance fitter was killed and an engineer injured when a large twin-arm dough-mixing machine fell from the forks of a fork lift truck. The machine was on the forks to enable maintenance work from beneath.

Case study 2
A worker received a serious hand injury when using a sharp knife to debone meat. The company now provides knife-proof arm guards and gloves for the non-knife hand and knife-proof aprons.

Further guidance

See HSE webpages on:

Food – 'struck by' www.hse.gov.uk/food/struckby.htm

Manual handling

Why manual handling is a priority

Manual handling injuries account for around a third of all injury reports to HSE in the food and drink industries. The majority of these injuries are caused when lifting or lowering loads, although the carrying and pushing / pulling of loads are also significant injury contributors.

Around a half of manual handling injuries are back injuries, primarily affecting the lower back.

Other common injuries are to the shoulders, frequently when lifting heavy or awkward objects above head height onto shelving or pallets.

A small percentage of injuries are due to related factors such as cuts from sharp edges or having fingers crushed by the load.

The law

The term manual handling not only covers the lifting, lowering and carrying of loads, but also includes the pushing and pulling of loads (eg wheeled trolleys and pump trucks).

The main requirements of the Manual Handling Operations Regulations 1992 are for employers to:

- **avoid** *hazardous* manual handling operations so far as is reasonably practicable.

If the load has to be handled, then you should:

- **assess** *hazardous* manual handling activities that cannot be avoided;
- **reduce** the risk of injury *so far as is reasonably practicable*.

How to manage the risks of manual handling

Assessing potentially hazardous manual handling activities
The temptation when assessing manual handling activities is to concentrate on the weight or the awkwardness of the load, without paying similar attention to the position from which you pick up or put down the load.

The Regulations do not specify any maximum or 'safe' weights. However, Figure 10 gives an approximate boundary within which the load is unlikely to create a risk, and therefore a detailed assessment should not be necessary.

The figure illustrates that a man lifting a 5 kg load from well in front of his feet is at a similar risk of injury to lifting 25 kg at table height. The weight / position combinations in the diagram can therefore be regarded as zones of equivalent risk.

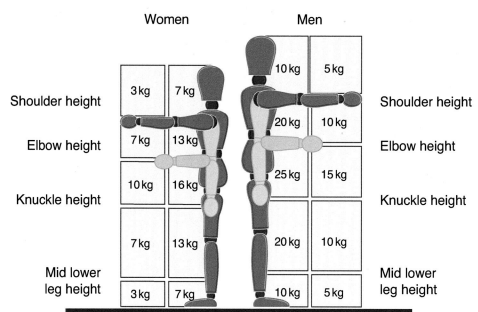

Figure 10 Weight / position combinations for women and men

Pushing and pulling loads

When pushing and pulling loads the most frequent injuries are back injuries. There are a variety of factors which affect the risk of pushing and pulling loads, and these are set out on HSE webpages at www.hse.gov.uk/msd/pushpull/risks.htm.

The effort needed to move a wheeled load depends not only on its weight and the floor slope, but also the condition of the wheels, their size and the floor smoothness. Larger wheels are easier to get rolling than smaller wheels and cope better with surface irregularities. Regular checking / maintenance is also important for wheeled trolleys, racks and roll cages, as if they have poorly maintained wheels they are much harder to steer and push / pull.

Key risk factors in manual handling assessments

Key factors to consider are:

- the weight of the load;
- the height at which the load will be picked up or placed – if practicable, avoid lifting heavy loads from the floor or very near the floor, or picking them up or placing them at a high level;
- preventing leaning sideways to pick up or put down loads, twisting the upper body or twisting and bending at the same time – these significantly increase the risk of back injury;
- whether there are any postural constraints, for example where it is difficult to adopt a good lifting posture due to load being in an awkward / restricted area, such as under a machine;
- how frequently loads have to be lifted, and how far they have to be carried;
- where the load is lifted from and is being put down. Good practice is to:
  - lift the load from close to the body (eg by pulling the load towards the body before lifting);
  - put down the load close to the body – and then reposition it away from the body if necessary by sliding it;
  - keep the path clear when carrying loads;
- load size / shape / grip – how easy it is to pick up and handle;
- the individual's capacity to safely lift the load. This will vary with factors such as:
  - the person's gender, height and strength;
  - how experienced they are at lifting heavy objects;
  - whether they have been trained to lift safely.

A very useful tool for the prioritisation and understanding of manual handling risks is HSE's MAC tool (Manual handling assessment charts). Using the tool one can break down tasks into discrete elements (using a camera's video function should be helpful for this) and score the elements depending on the risk. For more information on the MAC tool, see HSE webpages at www.hse.gov.uk/msd/mac/index.htm.

A checklist for manual handling

Good practice includes:

- Use lifting aids such as scissor lift tables, wheeled trolleys, pallet levellers, drum and reel lifters, vacuum lifters etc where practicable.
- Reduce the weight of the load and/or the vertical lift distance.
- Use intermediate bulk containers (IBCs) or bulk sacks instead of smaller containers and sacks which need to be manually handled.
- When stacking loads onto pallets, or destacking loads from pallets, put the pallet in use onto two disused pallets (see Figure 11), thereby raising it and reducing the amount of bending.
- Where there is a risk of over-filling trays or bins etc, mark the containers with a line to indicate the maximum load.
- Use smaller containers / shallower trays for product or end-of-line run-off etc to ensure they don't get too heavy.
- Move waste bins etc around on wheeled trolleys.
- When organising product on shelving, place heavier (and frequently picked) items at a height where there is less risk of injury (see Figure 11).
- Use counterbalances on heavy process vessel lids.
- Use bin lifters / tilters to avoid the need to bend to pick items from the bottom of large bins.
- Limit the stack height of empty pallets to make them easier to de-stack.
- Use high-visibility tape on walls to indicate maximum stack heights.
- Avoid using the highest or lowest racks on trolleys where the trays are heavy.

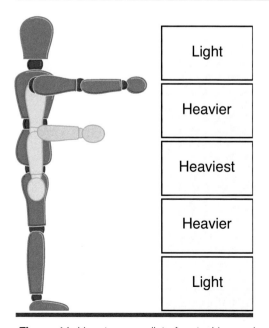

Figure 11 How to use pallets for stacking and organise product on shelving

---

Case studies

Case study 1
Preparing orders in a food warehouse involved lifting loads weighing up to 50 kg onto pallets. The bending, pulling and twisting required was causing many musculoskeletal injuries. The task was redesigned so that no heavy lifting above shoulder height was required and the maximum package weight was reduced to 25 kg. Injury rates decreased by 30% and costs reduced by 40%. Absenteeism went from 9% to 2% and the cost of implementation was recouped in 12 months.

Case study 2
Trays of pork cuts were stacked ten high and pushed on four-wheeled trolleys by production staff. Strains and sprains from pushing the trolleys were common, mainly due to damaged trolley wheels. The company implemented a trolley maintenance programme and employed a person whose main job was to repair, maintain and replace faulty wheels. There was a dramatic decrease in injuries, fewer staff complaints and an increase in productivity.

Further guidance

See HSE webpages on:

Manual handling and MSDs www.hse.gov.uk/msd/manualhandling.htm
Food industry manual handling www.hse.gov.uk/food/handling.htm
Occupational rehabilitation in the food manufacturing industry
www.hse.gov.uk/food/rehabilitation/index.htm

Also

Manual handling. Manual Handling Operations Regulations 1992 (as amended) L23
HSE Books 2004 www.hse.gov.uk/pubns/books/l23.htm
Manual handling at work – A brief guide INDG143 HSE Books 2012
www.hse.gov.uk/pubns/indg143.pdf
Manual handling assessment charts (the MAC tool) INDG383(rev2) HSE Books
2014 www.hse.gov.uk/pubns/indg383.htm
Moving food and drink: Manual handling solutions for the food and drink industries
HSG196 HSE Books 2000 www.hse.gov.uk/pubns/books/hsg196.htm

Upper limb disorders

Why upper limb disorders are a health priority

Upper limb disorders or ULDs are conditions which affect the muscles, tendons, ligaments, nerves or other soft tissues and joints in the neck, shoulders, arms, wrists, hands and fingers. They are often called repetitive strain injuries (RSIs), cumulative trauma disorder or occupational overuse syndrome. ULDs account for around one-quarter of reported occupational ill-health cases in the food and drink industries, however this is likely to be an underestimate due to the often progressive nature of the condition.

Some ULDs are recognised medical diseases and can be diagnosed as such by a doctor, for example carpal tunnel syndrome. However, other ULDs cannot be identified as a specific disease as, although there is pain, there may not be a clear underlying cause.

How to manage the risks of upper limb disorders

Recognising the symptoms

ULDs are a progressive condition that, if not identified early *and acted upon*, can lead to long-term disability in the affected area. Typical symptoms may include aching, discomfort or pain, tenderness, swelling, stiffness / impaired movement, tingling and numbness.

In the early stages the symptoms often disappear with rest. However, if the symptoms are ignored, they may become much worse, to the point where even light tasks at home or at work become difficult. If operators continue to work while suffering from ULDs, recovery can take years and some people will be left with a degree of permanent disability.

Identifying activities where ULDs may be a risk

Two ways of identifying ULD risks include looking at:

- accident and absence records to see whether there may be a history of ULDs;
- tasks with common risk factors which present a risk of ULDs. These risk factors include:
    - **Repetition** – performing the same motion or series of motions continually or very frequently, especially where there is a need to 'keep up' with the production line. Repetitive work can be seen in many food industries, for example on meat / poultry / fish processing and salad lines.
    - **Force required** – the amount of effort required to do a task – high force levels mean the muscles are in greater tension.
    - **Awkward or static posture** – movements of the hands, wrists or arms that are well outside their normal resting or 'comfortable' positions – sometimes referred to as 'out of neutral' positions. Although in everyday life we may have no problem with these 'awkward' positions, if these are combined with other risk factors such as high repetition, then they can significantly increase the risk of ULDs. Examples of awkward postures could be reaching to get something off a conveyor belt, raising elbows to around chest height, bending the wrist such that an obvious angle can be observed or gripping wide or very narrow objects. Examples of static postures could include leaning over a table or conveyor for long periods of time as it is not at the right height for the operator.
    - **Insufficient recovery time** – insufficient breaks may mean muscles are not given enough time to rest and recover. New starters may need additional breaks or more job rotation as they are particularly susceptible to ULDs as their muscles need time to build up strength and stamina.

HSE has produced a method of assessing tasks that require repetitive movement of the upper limbs; this can help prioritise ULD risks in the workplace. The Assessment of repetitive tasks (ART) tool is available free from the HSE website (www.hse.gov.uk/msd/uld/art/index.htm). Using the tool should help you to gain a greater understanding of the causes of ULDs and how to design work practices to minimise the risk.

Reducing the risk of ULDs

Where there is a potential for ULDs, and it is not reasonably practicable to automate the task, then consider the following to minimise the risk:

- Reduce the frequency of doing a task which may present a ULD risk by adding further tasks (job enlargement) to broaden the range of the work activity.
- Rotate higher risk tasks with other tasks. Note that job rotation:
    - must be done within a working day (not between days) – every two hours or so, or at break times, may be sufficient unless the risk is particularly high;

- must be managed – people should not be allowed to opt out;
  - may mean increasing the tasks done within a team, to allow for greater job rotation;
  - must include new starters and agency staff, who are often at the highest risk.
- Reduce the risk by improved workstation design:
  - ensure the workstation is at an appropriate height – provide stands for smaller workers where necessary;
  - design the workstation to minimise the amount of forward reaching and vertical hand movement – where possible try to avoid repetitive hand movements above shoulder height;
  - use trolleys, lift tables etc to minimise the amount of repetitive bending;
  - use product diverters on conveyor belts to bring product closer to operatives.
- Reduce the amount of force required to do the task.
- Pay special attention to those new to a task and new starters. They may be particularly vulnerable to ULDs as they need time to build up muscle strength and stamina. Note that in the first four–six weeks, new workers may need additional rotation and rest breaks until they build-up to normal work speeds.
- Proper maintenance and adjustment of machinery can be very important in minimising ULD risks. When machinery is not set up properly, or maintained, it can mean that operators further down the line have to work harder or faster, thereby increasing the likelihood of ULDs.
- Carefully review pre-commencement health questionnaires so that employees with past or existing conditions are not placed in jobs that are likely to aggravate them.

Figure 12 Working at a suitable height

Training and education

Training of operators: Operators should be aware that certain tasks could give rise to ULDs and what typical symptoms to look out for. The importance of reporting these symptoms immediately to management should be stressed.

Training of supervisors: Where ULDs could pose a risk, supervisors should be trained in the importance of preventing and managing ULDs. It is especially important that line management can pick up the early signs and make positive enquiries concerning ULD symptoms for those at higher risk, such as new starters.

Treatment and rehabilitation

The key to successful rehabilitation is early reporting of the symptoms and prompt action to significantly reduce or stop the exposure which caused them. For starters new to a task, mild aching and discomfort may not be unusual while their body gets used to the task. However, if this does not recover quickly with rest, or shows signs of getting worse, then their exposure to the task should be *significantly* reduced. If after a week or so the symptoms go away, then exposure to the task can be *gradually* increased over the coming weeks, but if the symptoms remain, then a complete rest from the task is likely to be necessary. Reintroduction from such a rest should be done gradually, with the aim of returning to normal working speeds / rotation patterns within four–six weeks.

There are no hard and fast rules about how much rest a person may need, or how long they will need to get back to normal working patterns. Indeed, some people may be particularly susceptible to ULDs and may never be able to return to the particular task. Individual cases must be closely monitored, with advice as necessary from an occupational health professional.

The use of wrist supports, anti-inflammatory drugs and pain killers should be avoided, as these may mask the symptoms, thereby running the risk of exacerbating or prolonging the condition. The '*work through the pain and you'll be all right*' treatment should never be dispensed by management.

Case study

ULD complaints were received from a few operatives who were hanging chickens. The task involved picking chickens up from a conveyor belt and hanging them by the legs onto a moving shackle line. This activity was done in a chilled environment for around six hours a day, with the longest continuous session being three hours. There were two separate hanging lines and conveyor belts, with three operators on each side who faced towards each other.

Observation of work method
Video analysis (see inset photo) showed that rather than hanging in front of him, one operator was reaching over to the right to hang the bird onto the shackle line (moving from right to left). This required more stretching, raising the arms higher and reaching across the body, all of which increase the risk of ULDs, as well as being a very inefficient technique.

Training new starters and retraining some existing operatives in an efficient hanging technique has reduced the risk of ULDs.

Improvements in workstation design

It was noticed that on one side the horizontal distance between the edge of the conveyor belt and the shackle line was some 110 mm further than the other. This meant that operators could not get as close to the shackle line and had to reach further and raise their arms higher to hang, increasing the risk of ULDs.

Reducing the horizontal distance from the conveyor edge to the shackle line to the same as the opposite side has reduced the risk of ULDs. For shorter operatives, the provision of operator stands has reduced the height of the shackle line relative to the body, further reducing the risk (repetitive movements of the hands above shoulder height increases the ULD risk).

Job design

Previously, rotation was only done at break times, so the operators could hang continuously for up to three hours.

After the assessment a buzzer was installed to signal the operators to move along one position every half hour, and the number of 'off-line' tasks which operators were trained to do was increased. This meant that the maximum continuous hanging time was reduced to 1.5 hours, and the minimum break from hanging would be 30 minutes, but is usually considerably longer.

No further complaints have been made after all the changes were brought in.

For further case studies, see:

www.hse.gov.uk/msd/uld/art/cartonassembly.htm
www.hse.gov.uk/msd/uld/art/croissant.htm

Further guidance

See HSE webpages on:

Musculoskeletal disorders www.hse.gov.uk/msd/index.htm
Food musculoskeletal disorders www.hse.gov.uk/food/musculoskeletal.htm
ULDs www.hse.gov.uk/msd/uld/index.htm
Assessment of repetitive tasks (ART) tool www.hse.gov.uk/msd/uld/art/index.htm
Occupational rehabilitation in the food industry
www.hse.gov.uk/food/rehabilitation/index.htm

Also

Managing upper limb disorders in the workplace – A brief guide INDG171(rev2) HSE Books 2013 www.hse.gov.uk/pubns/indg171.pdf

Occupational dermatitis

Why occupational dermatitis is a health priority

There are around 40 000 new cases of work-related dermatitis every year. Although these occur across a number of industries, the main causes of dermatitis are contact with soaps / cleaners and wet work, so the risk in the food and drink manufacturing industries, particularly, is high.

Types and causes of dermatitis

Most dermatitis affects the hands and arms as a result of contact with substances. There are two types of contact dermatitis:

Irritant contact dermatitis
This is a skin reaction leading to inflammation at the site of contact and can affect all workers. Causes include:

- wet work / exposure to detergents and cleaners;
- frequent hand washing / frequent use of alcohol-based sanitizers;
- contact with some foodstuffs (eg onions).

Contact dermatitis causes dry, red, itchy skin in the first instance. Swelling, scaling and blistering of the skin and pain may follow later. Repeated contact may lead to 'hyper-irritability' – the skin becomes inflamed more readily than normal and, in severe cases, can force workers to change jobs.

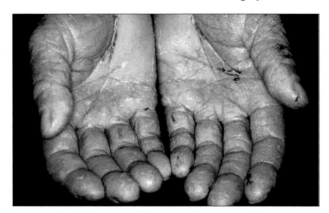

Wet work and exposure to detergents / cleaners account for the greater proportion of cases. The risk is significant when there are more than two hours' contact with water per day or 20 or more hand washes every day.

Figure 13 Irritant contact dermatitis

Allergic contact dermatitis
Allergic contact dermatitis (or skin sensitisation) is an immunological response to a sensitising substance (allergen). It affects specific workers who become sensitised to certain products and can be more difficult to control as very small exposures can trigger a reaction. Causes include:

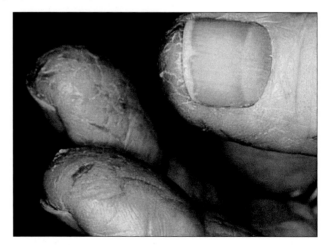

- shellfish, meat, poultry;
- flour;
- onions and garlic;
- herbs, seasoning and spices.

Figure 14 Allergic contact dermatitis from garlic

How to manage the risks of occupational dermatitis

Once a problem has been identified, possible remedies need to be considered. Exposure to hazardous materials by skin contact and absorption through the skin should be prevented or, where this is not reasonably practicable, adequately controlled.

Tasks where workers' hands come into contact with water, soaps, detergents and foodstuffs that can cause a reaction should be identified. Sickness absence due to skin problems should be monitored and workers' complaints investigated.

Adopting the **APC** approach can help in preventing dermatitis:

- **A**void or reduce contact with materials that cause skin / systemic problems.
- **P**rotect the skin.
- **C**heck for early signs of disease.

If a dermatitis problem is identified, the cause should be established and the following steps should be taken:

Avoid contact by elimination
Change the process by redesigning it in such a way as to eliminate and prevent direct contact. For example, this could involve redesigning the production process to reduce the need for hand washing.

Avoid contact by substitution
Substitute or replace the substance with something less harmful. Substituting the physical form of a substance may also reduce the potential for skin contact. Use granulated or liquid formulations rather than powders to reduce the spread of dusts.

Avoid or reduce contact by using engineering controls
Engineering controls include containment or enclosure of the substance. Partial enclosure with some form of LEV can also be very effective in controlling skin contact. However, there may remain potential for contact during cleaning, maintenance and repair operations.

Avoid or reduce contact by using a 'safe working distance'
The greater the distance between the worker and the hazardous substance, the less likely it is that contact will occur. Use tools to prevent prolonged contact with water or to reduce contact with irritant substances.

Avoid or reduce contact by using procedural controls
These controls might include, for example:

- using easy-to-clean work surfaces;
- spillage control procedures;
- avoiding processes where workers spend more than two hours in contact with water;
- less frequent hand washing, if hygiene controls allow;
- preventing or minimising access to areas where there is a risk of skin contact with substances.

Protect the skin by using personal protective equipment
Gloves can provide some protection from dermatitis but must be used with care and be suitable for the task. Wearing impermeable gloves for long periods can cause problems because of sweating inside the gloves. Latex gloves should be avoided because of the risk of allergy.

Protect using skin care products
Skin care products are designed to help maintain a stable and adequately hydrated barrier layer so the skin remains in good condition and retains its protective role. They are designed to be applied to the skin before the shift, at breaks and at the end of shift. Workers must be trained in how to apply these products properly.

A checklist for health surveillance

Skin checks are a crucial part of managing skin disease at work. Where there is a risk of dermatitis, workers should be trained in the control measures and a simple surveillance system should be set up so that workers and supervisors can spot the first signs of damage. Workers should also be trained in good skin care practices – such as correct use of hand washing and use of moisturisers at the end of the shift to replace essential oils in the skin – and the importance of reporting symptoms. The following questions will help form the basis of comprehensive health surveillance:

- Are there any processes where workers spend more than two hours in contact with water?
- Do hygiene controls mean that workers have to wash their hands frequently?
- Is there any evidence of dermatitis from exposure to produce or substances in the workplace?
- Can the harmful substances be replaced with safer alternatives?
- If not, can production be redesigned to minimise contact?
- Can the frequency of hand washing be reduced or contact with water minimised?
- If gloves have to be used to protect the skin, are the right gloves provided?
- Are workers trained in skin care procedures and the importance of reporting symptoms?
- Are supervisors trained to carry out regular skin checks?

Case studies

Case study 1
At a meat processor, workers who washed their hands up to 40 times a shift were affected by dermatitis. After a review, hand washing was reduced to 11 times per shift with no loss in hygiene. At the same time:

- the water temperature was adjusted;
- the chlorine dioxide dosing of the water supply was adjusted;
- a new food grade emollient cream to protect hands was introduced;
- vinyl gloves were provided. These improvements controlled the outbreak and also led to energy savings and improved quality control.

Case study 2
A number of employees in a food production area developed dermatitis. This was traced to water-disinfecting tablets which were used in water to wash vegetables. The employer stopped those who had developed dermatitis working in this area and issued suitable gloves to all the food handlers who were subsequently involved in the work. This satisfactorily resolved the problem.

Further guidance

See HSE webpages on:

Skin at work www.hse.gov.uk/skin/index.htm

Also

Managing skin exposure risks at work HSG262 HSE Books 2009
www.hse.gov.uk/pubns/books/hsg262.htm

Occupational asthma

Why occupational asthma is a health priority

About 35 000 workers across all industries suffer from work-related breathing / lung problems caused or made worse by work, with around 7000 new cases every year. Some will be suffering non-allergic disease such as chronic obstructive pulmonary disease (COPD) but a large number of cases will be work-related asthma. Exposure to flour dust is the second largest cause of occupational asthma.

Identifying cases of occupational asthma

Asthma
Identifying cases of occupational asthma can be difficult. Symptoms may be confused with other illnesses such as COPD. There may be a delay in the occurrence of symptoms for some hours after exposure so the link with work may not be obvious. Allergic occupational asthma occurs when workers become sensitised to particular dusts or aerosols that are breathed into their lungs. This is the cause for most cases of work-related asthma. There is usually a latency period between first exposure to the sensitiser and the onset of symptoms (which can be some years in the case of flour dust). However, once sensitised, exposure to very small amounts can trigger an attack.

Asthma causes chronic inflammation and constriction of the airways. It is a frightening condition and individual episodes can prove fatal.

Rhinitis
Rhinitis is an associated condition caused by chronic inflammation of the nasal mucous membranes from exposure to irritant dusts. This can result in a runny nose.

How to manage the risks of occupational asthma

Flour dust is probably the best known asthmagen in the food industry, but there are many other substances that have been identified including:

- flour dust and enzyme additives such as amylase;
- grain dust;
- egg protein;
- shellfish protein;
- fungal spores;
- some spices, vitamins and other additives;
- poultry dust.

Exposure to occupational asthmagens should be kept as low as reasonably practicable or ALARP. To manage the risks of occupational asthmagens you should:

- identify any potential asthmagens;
- where possible, avoid using the asthmagen, eg use non-stick surfaces rather than flour;
- substitute a safer substance if possible to remove the asthmagen;
- if the asthmagen cannot be removed use a less dusty form of the substance if one is available, eg pastes or liquid suspensions;
- prevent exposure by enclosing the process as much as possible. The aim should be to make sure that exposure is reduced below any WEL that has been set for the substance and. in all cases. to the lowest reasonably practicable level;

- use other forms of engineering controls such as local exhaust ventilation (LEV) if enclosure is not possible. LEV can be an effective control, but only if the equipment is correctly designed, installed and properly maintained and checked. Control measures such as LEV must be maintained in an effective state, in efficient working order and in good repair. This will include:
  - competent persons undertaking frequent visual checks;
  - examination and testing of LEV plant every 14 months (and a record kept for at least five years);
  - training employees in how to check and use the LEV effectively and knowing who to call if the LEV fails;

Figure 15 Hand-throwing flour raises dust

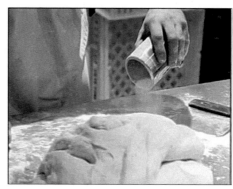

Figure 16 Using a dredger or sprinkler reduces dust levels considerably

Figure 17 Using a vacuum cleaner to clean up flour spillage

Figure 18 Dust extraction at flour sack-tip point

- as a last resort, use respiratory protective equipment (RPE) for certain operations; however, RPE should not be the primary means of control. If RPE has to be used as part of the overall control process, it must be suitable and manufactured to an appropriate standard. Before using any tight-fitting mask (including disposable masks), a face-fit test for the individual worker must be carried out by a competent face-fit tester. Workers and supervisors should be properly trained in its use and supervised. If the equipment is reusable, it should be regularly cleaned and checked to ensure that it remains effective and is replaced when necessary. Written records of monthly RPE maintenance must be kept;
- have in place a procedure for cleaning any spillages. To clean up spilt dust, a Type H (HEPA filter) vacuum cleaner should be used. Dust must not be cleaned up using dry-brushing or blowing down techniques;
- carry out monitoring of dust levels and health surveillance such as lung function testing to detect workers who are being affected at an early stage.

A checklist for health surveillance

Where workers are regularly exposed to asthmagens and other agents causing lung disease, the employer must provide health surveillance to detect early symptoms of disease, usually through questionnaires and spirometry. Ask the following questions:

- Is it possible to substitute your asthmagens for safer substances?
- If not, is it possible to prevent inhalation of dust, aerosols or fumes by better containment or other engineering controls?
- Is there a cleaning system which prevents escape of dust – for example, using HEPA-filtered vacuum cleaners instead of dry-brushing or blowing down?
- If LEV is used, has it been professionally designed and installed? Is there a plan for regular maintenance and inspection?
- If RPE has to be used as part of the overall control process, are there sufficient supplies of suitable RPE and are workers trained in its use? Is face-fit testing done to make sure it works for all workers and is RPE regularly maintained and replaced?
- Are dust levels monitored and is health surveillance carried out?

Case studies

Case study 1
A 50-year-old female worker who had worked in a small craft bakery all her working life developed what she thought was a wheezy bronchitis. Her work involved making bread and cakes and she was the only baker in the bakery apart from the owner. The woman visited her GP who diagnosed occupational asthma and she was unable to continue her employment at the bakery due to her condition.

Case study 2
A 20-year-old man was admitted to hospital from work with an acute asthmatic attack caused by flour dust inhalation. In the previous 12 months he had been absent from work for 25 days with chest symptoms. The company introduced new engineering controls and better work methods. His exposure to flour dust was dramatically reduced and he was able to go back to work. In the following three years he did not have any time off with chest problems.

Further guidance

See HSE webpages on:

Asthma www.hse.gov.uk/asthma/index.htm
Personal protective equipment (PPE) www.hse.gov.uk/coshh/basics/ppe.htm

Also

Bakers – time to clear the air INDG429 HSE Books 2009
www.hse.gov.uk/pubns/indg429.pdf

Available from the Federation of Bakers (www.bakersfederation.org.uk):

Guidance on dust control and health surveillance in bakeries (2008)
Breathe easy (2008) Training DVD programme on controlling dust in bakeries
A baker's dozen – Thirteen essentials for health and safety in bakeries

Noise-induced hearing damage

Why noise-induced hearing damage is a health priority

Over one million workers are exposed to excessive noise and over 17 000 people suffer deafness or tinnitus (permanent, disabling ringing in the ears) caused by noise exposure at work.

Loud noise can also increase the risk of accidents as it masks safety warnings and causes fatigue and loss of concentration.

There are many potentially noisy processes in the food and drink industries.

The law

The Control of Noise at Work Regulations 2005 require employers to eliminate or reduce the risks to health from noise. This involves eliminating noise at source or, where this is not reasonably practicable, reducing the level so far as is reasonably practicable or SFAIRP.

The Regulations set two exposure levels:

- a lower exposure action level of 80 dB at which workers need to be informed about risks to their hearing and be provided with hearing protectors if they want them;
- an upper exposure level of 85 dB at which noise exposure has to be controlled by doing all that is reasonably practicable other than by hearing protection, for example by making machinery quieter or soundproofing. Where this is not possible, hearing protection zones need to be set up and clearly marked and hearing protection worn. Additionally, health surveillance is required where workers are at risk.

How to manage the risks from exposure to noise

Reducing noise at source
Noise from machinery and plant can be reduced by:

- purchasing machinery / plant designed to emit as low a noise level as possible;
- segregating noisy machinery / plant from workers (eg in another room);
- soundproofing enclosure of the machinery / plant;
- lining guards / panels with noise-damping material;
- lining the inside of hoppers with impact-deadening material;
- fitting devices such as anti-vibration mounts, air pressure regulators, pneumatic exhaust silencers etc;
- regular maintenance.

Hearing protection
Hearing protection is not a substitute for reducing exposure. In selecting the right type of hearing protection, consider the following:

- hearing protection should reduce individual workers' exposure below a daily dose of 87 dB even in the noisiest of workplaces and preferably to between 70 and 80 dB;
- comfort and hygiene;
- protectors which block too much sound can make communication difficult and may cause safety risks (for example, inability to hear vehicles moving nearby);
- workers may need training to ensure they use the protection properly;
- supervision in use of protection in areas where the upper exposure action level is exceeded;

- protection needs to be maintained and replaced when damaged.

Noise doses, levels and exposure times

When calculating the noise dose it is necessary to take account of both the noise level and the time that the workers are exposed. The daily personal noise exposure action levels are eight-hour time-weighted averages. So, exposure to:

- 83 dB for four hours is equivalent to 80 dB for eight hours;
- 92 dB for only half an hour is also equivalent to 80 dB for eight hours;
- <80 dB over long shifts or through overtime can also be equivalent to 80 dB for eight hours (eg 79 dB for ten hours or 78 dB for 12 hours).

The decibel scale is a logarithmic scale. This means that 90 dB sounds twice as loud as 80 dB but contains ten times more energy. An increase of 3 dB in noise level is only just audible but it is a doubling of the noise energy.

Drinks	dB
Bottling halls	85–95
Bottle filling / labelling	85–95
De-crating / washing	85–96
Casking / kegging	85–100
Cooperage machines	>95
Meat	
Animals in lairage	80–110
Powered saws	up to 100
Blast-freezers / chillers	85–107
Bowl-choppers	>90
Packing machinery	85–95
Milling	
Mill areas	85–95
Hammer mills	95–100
Grinders	85–95
Seed graders	90
Bagging lines	85–90
Bakery	
Dough-mixing room	85
Baking plant	85
De-panning	90
Bread slicing	85–90
Fruit washing	92
Dairy	
Production areas	85–95
Homogenisers	90–95
Bottling lines	90–95
Blast-chillers	87–95
Pneumatics	85–95
Confectionery	
Hopper feed	95
Mould-shakers	90–95
Wrap / bagging	85–95
High boiling	85

Figure 19 Typical noise levels in food and drink industries

A checklist for health surveillance

Where workers are regularly exposed to noise above the upper exposure action level, the employer must provide audiometry to test their hearing and detect early symptoms of hearing damage. Ask the following questions:

● Have you assessed your premises to identify potentially noisy areas or processes?
● Have you made a more detailed assessment (including measurement as appropriate) where it is possible that the action levels are exceeded?
● Do you specify noise reduction requirements when purchasing new machinery or plant?
● What can be done to reduce noise levels at source (through consultation with workers and their safety representatives)?
● Do you consult with workers and safety representatives on hearing protection measures?
● Do you provide suitable hearing protection in areas where the lower exposure action level is exceeded?
● Have you identified areas where wearing of hearing protection is compulsory because the upper exposure action level is exceeded?
● Do you make arrangements for health surveillance / audiometry testing for workers who are at risk or who regularly work in areas where the upper exposure action level is likely to be exceeded?

Figure 20 Testing for hearing damage using audiometry

Case studies

Case study 1
In a sandwich-making factory in the Midlands, sandwich cutter machines produced noise levels of 95 dB. The noise was caused by heavy metal arms which drove the reciprocating blade on the machines. The engineer developed an alternative linkage using flexible nylon straps. This reduced noise levels to 75 dB, removing the need for hearing protection to be worn. In addition, the new strap required significantly less maintenance and repair.

Case study 2
Glass jars were transported along a conveyor from the jar cleaner to the filler. The glass jars clashed together producing noise levels of 96 dB. An enclosure was put over the conveyor at a cost of £2000 and the conveyor speed was changed to reduce jar clashing. Noise levels reduced to 86 dB.

Case study 3
A soft drinks factory used a large air compressor, air from which was used to operate machines on the bottling line. The air compressor was located in the middle of the production area and produced noise levels of 94–95 dB. The company moved the air compressor out of the production hall into a nearby enclosed and unmanned room, eliminating the noise source.

Further guidance

See HSE webpages on:

Main noise www.hse.gov.uk/noise/index.htm
Food noise www.hse.gov.uk/food/noise.htm

Also

Sound solutions for the food and drink industries: Reducing noise in food and drink manufacturing HSG232 HSE Books 2013
www.hse.gov.uk/pubns/books/hsg232.htm

Work-related stress

Why work-related stress is a health priority

No data is available for the prevalence of work-related stress in the food and drink manufacturing industries. However, work-related stress is often cited as a cause of mental ill health. HSE figures show that, nationally, stress-related illnesses are among the most common work-related illnesses and that over 10 million working days are lost every year. Reports from the Food Industry Medical Association in 2005 suggested that mental illness associated with stress was responsible for almost as much absence as back pain and that mental ill health accounted for around 30% of cases of occupational ill health in food and drink manufacture.

How to manage the risk of work-related stress

Stress is a significant occupational health risk. There is a clear link between poor work organisation and subsequent ill health.

Pressure in itself is not necessarily bad and many people thrive on it. It is when pressure experienced by an individual exceeds their ability to cope with it that ill-health problems can result.

Work-related stress caused by excessive work demands, lack of control over work etc is often cited as a cause of mental ill health.

It is important to have a clear Stress Policy which focuses on:

- prevention;
- assessment of risk;
- recognition of symptoms;
- causes of stress;
- clear process for managing any cases;
- risk assessment at the individual person level.

Effective management training covering these topics will certainly help any organisation.

The HSE Management Standards identify six aspects of work and workplace relationships which can contribute to the risk of work-related stress:

- **Demand** – issues like workload, work pattern and the work environment.
- **Control** – how much say the person has about the way they do their work.
- **Support** – including the encouragement, sponsorship and resources provided by the employer, line management and colleagues.
- **Relationships** – including promoting positive working to avoid conflict and dealing with unacceptable behaviour.
- **Role** – whether people understand their role within the organisation and whether the organisation ensures that the person does not have conflicting roles.
- **Change** – how organisational change (large or small) is managed and communicated in the organisation, including training to support changes.

A checklist for individual stress risk assessments

Consider the following impacts when carrying out individual stress risk assessments:

- **Work performance** – increased absence levels, reduced productivity, unexplained errors, resistance to change, lack of concentration.
- **Behavioural impact** – changes in behaviour, withdrawn, aggressive, emotional outbursts, interpersonal conflict.
- **Physical impact** – fatigue, headaches, weight loss / gain, stomach complaints, chest pains, nausea / sickness, sleep problems, changes in appearance.

In completing an individual's stress risk assessment take into account:

- what the individual (and yourself) considers is causing their stress (compare this against the six HSE Management Standards, above);
- what impact the stress has had on the individual (compare against the three impact headings, above).

Then consider:

- What steps are currently taken to help deal with the stress?
- What control / support measures are in place?
- What extra help or support is required which would make a difference?
- How will you monitor improvements against the above impacts?

Both parties should then meet to discuss their views and agree what actions are to be taken, by whom and by when. In addition, how they will both monitor and review the situation in the future.

Case study

An office worker developed physical ill health (chest complaint) that proved resistant to usual GP treatment and was absent for three weeks with potential for long-term absence. During this time he was referred to the company's occupational health department and it was established that a combination of personal and work pressures had affected his physical resilience. Previously, the worker had a good attendance record.

An individual stress risk assessment was completed and a discussion on the findings held between the employee and his manager in the presence of an independent mediating manager. Recommendations included reducing overtime and out-of-hours work and meals / breaks to be taken away from the worker's desk. Weekly occupational health support was also offered. The employee returned to work and, within two weeks of working to the advice given, showed improvement to both performance and physical health.

Further guidance

See HSE webpages on:

Tackling work-related stress www.hse.gov.uk/stress/

Food and Drink Manufacture Health and Safety Forum

What is the Forum?

The Forum is a tripartite committee comprising the main food and drink trade associations and trades unions along with representatives from HSE's Food and Drink Manufacture Section and IOSH's Food and Drink Group.

The Forum was established in 2004 and holds meetings twice a year to discuss, prioritise and drive forward a range of health and safety initiatives to reduce injuries and occupational ill health in the industry.

The Forum works with IOSH to organise the annual National Food and Drink Manufacture Health and Safety Conference.

Member organisations of the Forum:

Food and Drink Federation
British Poultry Council
Meat Joint Working Party
Pet Food Manufacturers' Association
Dairy UK
Federation of Bakers
National Association of Master Bakers
Chilled Food Association
British Frozen Food Federation
Agricultural Industries Confederation
British Beer and Pub Association
British Soft Drinks Association
Scotch Whisky Association
Maltsters' Association of Great Britain
USDAW (Union of Shop, Distributive and Allied Workers)
GMB (general workers' union)
BFAWU (Bakers, Food and Allied Workers' Union)
UNITE (transport and general workers' union)
Health and Safety Executive – Manufacturing Sector
Institute of Occupational Safety and Health (IOSH) – Food and Drink Group

What does the Forum do?

The Forum:

- brings its experience to bear to determine the best ways to further reduce injuries and occupational ill health in the food and drink manufacturing industries;
- seeks to act as a catalyst for positive change, evaluating new and original ideas in addition to tried and tested methods;
- encourages member organisations to adopt, promote and support best practice and initiatives agreed by the Forum;
- seeks to work together in the spirit of joint working, using all communication opportunities;
- acts as a catalyst for workplace-level partnerships.

Member organisations of the Forum have agreed a 'Common strategy' (www.hse.gov.uk/food/common-strategy.pdf) setting out the actions each party will undertake to further reduce injuries and occupational ill health.

Further information

For information about health and safety, or to report inconsistencies or inaccuracies in this guidance, visit www.hse.gov.uk/. You can view HSE guidance online and order priced publications from the website. HSE priced publications are also available from bookshops.